TABLE
STYLINGS

TABLE STYLINGS

INSPIRATIONAL SETTINGS AND
DECORATIVE THEMES FOR YOUR TABLE

———

TESSA EVELEGH

LORENZ BOOKS

First published in 1999 by Lorenz Books

© Anness Publishing Limited 1999

Lorenz Books is an imprint of Anness Publishing Limited, Hermes House, 88–89, Blackfriars Road, London SE1 8HA

Published in the USA by Lorenz Books, Anness Publishing Inc., 27 West 20th Street, New York, NY 10011; (800) 354-9657

Distributed in Canada by Raincoast Books, 8680 Cambie Street, Vancouver, British Columbia V6P 6M9

A CIP catalogue record for this book is available from the British Library

ISBN 0 7548 0196 9

PUBLISHER: Joanna Lorenz

EDITOR: Emma Gray

DESIGNER: Nigel Partridge

PHOTOGRAPHY: Polly Wreford

ADDITIONAL PROJECTS BY: Jane Newdick (Easter Festivity, Thanksgiving), Andrea Spencer

(White Magic, Simply Natural, Fun with Colour, Modern Christmas, Shaker Styling)

Published as an extract from a larger book, *Table Settings*

Printed and bound in Singapore

1 3 5 7 9 10 8 6 4 2

CONTENTS

ELEMENTS
OF STYLE

The first step towards creating beautiful table settings is to consider the separate elements, such as china, glass and cutlery, and how they interact.

TABLE MANNERS

Much of the enjoyment of inviting friends and family to join you for a meal is the pleasure of preparing it, of making the table and room look appealing, as well as cooking the delicious food. A beautifully laid table provides an inviting ambience that welcomes guests and sets off the meal. The basic ingredients of crisp linen, fine china, glass and cutlery are always there, but with imagination they can be treated in different ways. The fold of the napkins, the choice of serving dishes, flowers, candles and candlesticks, and the presentation of the food all affect the overall look of the table. The ideas throughout this book do not require you to buy expensive pieces of tableware, or to follow formal rules of table etiquette. Using everyday items and a basic dinner service, you can create very different settings to suit the mood and the occasion, and to lend an individual feel to your table.

Etiquette is really another word for manners, which are simply a set of rules developed so that everyone instinctively knows what to do in certain situations and can therefore be

ABOVE: Traditional silver-plated cutlery is still a popular choice today.

comfortable within the group. Manners are constantly changing, however, and social etiquette is no longer as rigid as it used to be. The overriding point of good manners is to be considerate to others and to make them feel at ease, and this is no less true at the table.

In Edwardian times, the elaborate utensils and a complicated code of behaviour had turned formal mealtimes into a trial for many, especially if they were not in their usual social circle. Thankfully, this has all but disappeared, and cutlery and china are far simpler. Mixing and matching china and linens is now acceptable, offering scope for creating imaginative and individual table settings.

BELOW: Decorate the table for special occasions such as Valentine's Day.

PLACE SETTINGS

Sitting down to a table laid with a plate and a battery of utensils for each person is a modern innovation. In the fifteenth century, there were no forks; only knives and spoons were used. Once the fork arrived, a whole range of utensils was designed for use with different foods. These included fish knives and forks, soup spoons, pickle forks, cake knives and jam spoons.

Formal tables are laid according to tradition, the purpose behind the ordered positioning of all the items being the smooth running of the meal. Cutlery should be laid on either side of the plates so that implements for the first course are on the outside. Dessert spoons and forks may be placed on either side or above. It is correct to set all the glasses to the right, above the knives, before the meal begins; they may be removed later on.

More informal meals do not have to adhere rigidly to the rules: indeed, many restaurants "break the rules" to create more imaginative place settings. For a special occasion, tie cutlery with a gold ribbon and lay them diagonally across the plate, or stand them upright in a glass tumbler. Knives, forks and spoons are very sculptural shapes that can be accentuated by making them the centre of attention.

ABOVE: *Napkins add a note of elegance to each place setting.*

BELOW: *Cutlery is placed in order of the courses, from outside in.*

BELOW: *Plan the cutlery for each stage of the meal.*

FEEDING THE SENSES

A beautifully laid table, decorated with candles and with a bowl of fruit or scented flowers, appeals to our senses of sight and smell. When we unfold a crisp linen napkin or pick up a wine glass, our sense of touch also comes to life. Whether the dinner service is delicate porcelain or rugged earthenware, we appreciate and savour these different textures, contrasted with the cool cutlery sparkling in the candlelight. Enjoying a meal is a total experience, involving all our senses to make a pleasing and harmonious blend of elements.

Depending on the occasion, choose some elements of the table for their texture as well as their colour. Hessian table mats and rustic pottery would be ideal for a simple meal of cheese and pâté served on a wooden table. Silver

ABOVE: Give extra texture to napkins by adding matching chenille tassels.

ABOVE: Decorate glass with hand-painted designs in white and gold.

LEFT: Rugged earthenware pottery mixes well with natural linen.

RIGHT: Clear acrylic resin cutlery handles give a clean modern look to a table.

cutlery and a white tablecloth have quite a different feel, suitable for a more formal occasion.

A glass bowl of water decorated with a floating candle and a few petals, or a single flower head, gives an extra dimension to the table. Add some coloured glass pebbles or pretty seashells to the bottom of the bowl on some occasions, to keep the idea fresh.

Flowers are, of course, a favourite way to bring scent, colour and texture to a table. For variety, try arrangements of flowers such as gerberas or sunflowers for a family meal, or gilded leaves and berries for a dinner party. Vegetables such as squashes (gourds) or artichokes make excellent table decorations to awaken your guests' senses as well as their tastebuds.

CHINA

This single element creates the greatest impact on table settings – not just in terms of colour and pattern, but in the material it is made of and in the shape of the designs. Many people build up two dinner services – an elegant design for dinner parties, and a more everyday set for family meals. But this need not limit you to just these two table-setting looks; you can use them as a framework around which to build endless styles to suit many different occasions.

To extend your range of options for entertaining, you could buy some pretty hand-painted soup bowls or

ABOVE: A blue and white patterned dinner service such as Spode's willow pattern is a perennial favourite. The beauty of these traditional designs is that they can be mixed and matched.

some side plates to co-ordinate with either of your main dinner services. Or you could add a large item such as a beautiful salad bowl, dessert dish or soup tureen to give your table an elegant new look. Bearing this in mind, choose the main dinner set very carefully in a colour and pattern that you will not tire of easily, but will continue to love for many years.

BELOW: Textured patterns make cream and white china more interesting. Again, you can successfully mix and match different designs when you want to add an extra piece to your dinner service.

ABOVE: The fine texture of traditional porcelain means it can be shaped into the most delicate designs. This tea cup and saucer have an exquisite translucent quality.

CUTLERY

The battery of cutlery that is now available is quite a recent innovation. Dinner forks for use at meals did not appear until the sixteenth century but, once they did so, it seems there was no looking back. By Edwardian times, there were mealtime tools available for every imaginable use, including intricately patterned fish knives, servers, cake forks with cutting edges and long-handled pickle forks.

Table etiquette was very precise during this period, and the right equipment had to be used. Formal cutlery, with several sizes of knife, fork and spoon, is still available, including serving spoons, soup spoons, butter knives and steak knives, but nowadays most everyday sets simply consist of basic knives, forks, spoons and teaspoons.

Traditionally, formal cutlery was made of silver, although much of it was plated. The knives, and sometimes the forks, often had handles made of a different material, such as bone, horn or wood. The Victorians initiated a fashion for making elaborate special-use cutlery, which was sometimes intricately engraved and fitted with handles in valuable materials such as mother-of-pearl. Very special sets of coffee spoons were even given a silver-gilt lining to their bowls.

Most modern cutlery is now made of one piece of stainless steel and is completely dishwasher-proof. However, a few beautiful pieces of antique serving cutlery, although less resilient, greatly enhance a table setting for a special occasion.

ABOVE: *Attractive cutlery deserves to be shown off, and a buffet table offers plenty of scope.*

LEFT: *Lend interest to empty plates by laying cutlery tied with a flamboyant bow in the centre.*

RIGHT: *Wooden handles become wonderfully smoothed and polished with age, developing a patina that is hard to match in any other cutlery.*

GLASS

The glorious reflective quality of glass-ware brings sparkle to every table setting. The more facets it offers to the light, the more sparkle it brings. With the dancing light of reflected candle flames, it helps lend a diamond-like shimmer to the table. Uncut glass adds to the table, but in a quite modern, uncluttered way that some people believe is more elegant.

BELOW: A witty modern decoration for a decanter is a "necklace" of chandelier crystals and feathers.

ABOVE: Glass lends height and sparkle. Choose shapes that complement your dinner service.

BELOW: An elegant way to decorate pre-dinner glasses is to wrap them with skeletonized magnolia leaves.

At its simplest, glassware is represented by a single tumbler placed at the guest's right hand; for a formal dinner, this can grow to a whole group, preferably from the same glass service though in different but related shapes. These stand like a family at each place setting, gathered above the blades of the knives. If space is limited on the table, extra glasses can be added when required.

LINEN

Beautiful table surfaces deserve to be shown off and, in such circumstances, it is quite correct to forgo a tablecloth, using place mats instead. For formal dinners, tradition demands that a tablecloth is white, preferably linen, and is draped to hang halfway down to the floor. More informally, sheets, bedcovers or any other length of cloth, even a sari, can be used to widen the repertoire for an imaginatively dressed table. Napkins may or may not match the tablecloth, and can be an art form in their own right.

RIGHT: Damask, with its glorious interwoven designs, can be made of silk or heavy cotton.

BELOW: This unusual napkin ring is made of a leather thong and a bone toggle.

BELOW: This napkin is actually a linen tea towel (dish cloth), which has been used to tie a soup bowl and plate.

BELOW: Here, a leather thong is bound round natural linen, then trimmed with feathers.

CANDLES

Candles are the most beautiful form of table lighting, casting a natural and flattering glow over the table and the faces of the diners. Their dancing flames have a beguiling quality that no light bulb could begin to imitate, and their evocative waxy aroma instantly creates a truly romantic ambience. Scented candles will enhance the mood even further.

Candles come in many shapes and forms, but even with ordinary tapered candles you can create many different looks to suit the table setting. Colour

co-ordinate them with the tablecloth or china and put them in holders that are in keeping with the overall style. Be sure to position the candles where they will not irritate your guests.

LEFT: The evocative natural aroma of beeswax makes these golden candles universally appealing.

RIGHT: Decorating a candelabra with crystal drops immediately gives it a dressed-up evening look.

BELOW: Pretty floating flower candles are enhanced by the real thing in an elegant glass tazza.

THE TABLE
STYLINGS

These imaginative ideas will transform your table and delight your guests.
Create lovely settings to reflect the seasons and to celebrate family occasions.

WHITE MAGIC

Translucent organdie gives a crisp and airy look to this most elegant of table settings. The gracefully curved shapes of the china and glass echo the curves of a pewter dish and two pewter jugs (pitchers). The white amaryllis blooms set into one of the jugs form a dramatic floral centrepiece for the table, yet could not be easier to put in place. The curves and points of their spectacular petals echo the flowing lines of the plate edgings.

Delicate detailing on glassware and napkins is set against the smooth lines of the main pieces. The glasses and matching decanter are decorated with tracery lines in white, then given added sparkle with a little diamanté. The napkins are tied with white gauzy ribbon, and the final touch is provided by organdie party favours filled with pot-pourri and tied with diamanté-decorated ribbons for guests to take home at the end of the meal as souvenirs.

RIGHT: Painted glasses and organdie sachets filled with pot-pourri perfectly complement pure white and pewter.

SPARKLING GLASSES

Decorated glasses add a very special touch to a celebration table setting. Hand-painted with white matt emulsion (latex), the patterns will easily wash off; for a more permanent effect,

use glass paint. If you are a little less than confident about painting the glasses freehand, draw out the pattern on a piece of paper first, then slip this inside each glass and paint over the lines.

MATERIALS
stemmed glasses
white matt emulsion (latex) or
glass paint
small artist's paintbrush
tweezers
all-purpose glue
diamanté stones

1 Holding the glass by the stem, paint sweeping lines and curves with an artist's paintbrush. Leave to dry.

2 Use tweezers to dab a little glue on to the back of each diamanté stone laid face down on a fingertip. Carefully press on to the glass.

ORGANDIE SACHETS

These sachets will scent the air during the meal and make welcome party favours to take home.

MATERIALS
organdie
pinking shears
pot-pourri
fine wire
rayon ribbon
diamanté stones
all-purpose glue

NAPKIN TIE: Delicate organdie napkins are tied with gauzy white ribbon trimmed with diamanté stones.

1 Cut a circle of organdie, and fill the centre with pot-pourri. Draw the organdie together around the filling.

2 Wind fine wire around the sachet to secure it. Tie on a length of ribbon and glue on some diamanté stones.

THE MIDAS TOUCH

Add a little gold to anything and it immediately becomes very special indeed, but pile it on too keenly and the final effect can be overpowering. The best solution is to mix the metals, using brass, pewter and even tarnished silver. If your household posessions do not stretch to all these, try a length of gold organza trimmed with gold furnishing braid as an overcloth. Gold-rimmed glasses and remnants of brocade made into matching napkins are two inexpensive ways to add just enough glitz to a table.

Take a tip from the gilders of old, who used to apply gold leaf over a base of ox-blood red, deep turquoise or ochre. Here the colour scheme is based on turquoise, with a silk sari providing the undercloth. Use picture framer's gilt wax to add a glint to a flower arrangement or a dish of pears for a dramatic golden centrepiece.

RIGHT: Glowing candlelight brings out the opulent warmth and golden colours of this festive table setting.

GOLD-RICH TABLE LINEN

Gold metal-shot organza is not expensive and, if you use it as an overcloth, you do not need a large amount. It immediately brings the gold touch to any table setting, looking especially rich when placed over slubbed silk or a sari, as here.

MATERIALS
gold metal-shot organza
scissors
damp cloth
iron
needle
thread
gold furnishing braid to trim the organza, plus an additional 15cm/6in for the corners

1 Cut a piece of gold organza slightly smaller than the tablecloth you will use underneath.

2 Make a fine rolled hem along the edges. On a low heat and with a damp cloth between the iron and organza, press the seams flat.

3 Slip stitch the braid into place along the edges of the organza. At the corners, twist the braid to form a small loop. Stitch the braid to the tablecloth and itself, where it crosses.

VELVET TIES: A remnant of furnishing brocade, which has been cut into napkin-sized pieces and then hemmed on all four sides, becomes rich table linen. Add the finishing touch by choosing two tones of narrow velvet ribbon that match the brocade napkins. Cut each end of the ribbons at an angle, then tie them together around the centre of the napkin.

GILDED CENTREPIECE

To complement the richness of a gold table scheme, take rust-coloured flowers and add your own golden touch. This low bowl of calla lilies and tree ivy provides an easy-to-make, yet gloriously golden centrepiece for a special dinner table.

MATERIALS
scissors
florist's foam
shallow metal bowl
picture framer's gilt wax
12 calla lilies
small bunch of tree ivy, with berries

1 Cut the florist's foam to fit snugly inside the metal bowl, then soak it in water. Use the picture framer's gilt wax to gild the lilies and ivy. Cut the stems short, then push them into the florist's foam so that the lily flowers all face outwards.

2 Use the ivy to fill the gaps in the arrangement, pushing each sprig firmly into the foam.

GILDED PEARS: Simply rub gilt wax over a pear and terracotta pot.

FUN WITH COLOUR

—

Create the brightest of table settings by choosing strong and clashing colours: fuchsia pink and orange, turquoise blue and yellow. The art is in not being afraid to throw in all the colours while keeping them close in tone. The look is fun and very modern with vibrant colours and organic free-form shapes.

With all this colour, it is wise to keep the setting clean and free of pattern. Let stylized flower and leaf card (card stock) shapes and ric-rac (rick rack) ties break up solid blocks of colour. Choose daisy-like gerberas for a floral centrepiece, and display in a brilliantly coloured enamel pitcher for an exuberant effect. This is a style in which you could introduce a touch of fun by placing a child's lollipop with each bundle of cutlery. The waxy texture and look of coloured candles is the perfect accessory for this table. Again, choose simple shapes in strong colours.

RIGHT: Flamboyant colour can be intensified by adding yet more extrovert shades with flowers and other accessories.

ZANY PAPER

1 Cut a gift tag from coloured card (card stock). Draw a leaf shape on to the card. Punch a hole in the card. Cut out most of the design and push it out from the background.

2 Wrap the gift and bind with ric-rac braid. Thread the tag on to the ric-rac and tie to secure.

FIND YOUR PLACE: *Make place cards by cutting shapes from coloured card. Write on each guest's initial in brightly coloured ink.*

Good giftwrap does not have to be expensive. Tissue paper and coloured newspaper (search international news stalls for the greatest choice) make perfect wrapping papers, especially when they are accessorized by brightly coloured home-made cards and eye-catching ric-rac ties in fantastically vivid contrasting colours.

MATERIALS
coloured card (card stock)
scissors
pencil
hole punch
craft knife and cutting mat
tissue paper or coloured newspaper
contrasting ric-rac braid

COLOUR CONTRASTS

1 Punch holes in the felt to make spots. Draw a stylized fern shape in pencil on paper, then cut it out and use it as a template to cut out the fern shape from felt. Stick the felt fern on to one corner of the napkin, using fabric glue. Stick the felt spots around the edge of the napkin to make a border.

FLOATING FLOWER: For a lovely fresh decoration, float a single flower head in a clear glass bowl of water.

Appliqué does not necessarily mean tricky needlework. Using simple felt shapes, it can be very quick and easy. These felt spots and the felt fern shape are stuck on using fabric glue. If you prefer, you can secure each spot with a tiny stitch and the fern with a stitch at each point.

MATERIALS
felt
hole punch
pencil
paper
scissors
napkins in pink and turquoise
fabric glue

CROSS-STITCH HEARTS

One of the simplest stitches used in embroidery is cross-stitch. Here, it used to depict a Shaker heart on plain-coloured napkins. Either use ready-made napkins, or take squares of linen or cotton fabric and hem the edges.

MATERIALS
pencil
tissue paper
dressmaker's pins
napkins
needle and embroidery thread (floss)
scissors

1 Draw a heart shape in evenly-sized crosses on the tissue paper. Pin the tissue paper to the napkin, then stitch over the crosses. Make three crosses on each side of the corner.

2 Carefully tear away the tissue paper, leaving the cross-stitch motifs. If any small pieces of paper remain caught under the stitches, use the point of the needle to remove them.

CANDLE-WRAP: *Plain white candles are stored in a traditional wooden candlebox. Embellish them with a wide strip of check fabric held in place with narrow linen tape.*

METAL HEARTS

Aluminium (tooling) foil, which is available in rolls from specialist art shops, is strong yet easy to cut. Here, it is transformed into delightful heart-embossed napkin rings, using just an ordinary dressmaker's pin to pierce the foil. A packaging tube makes a mould for the rings.

MATERIALS
1m/1yd aluminium foil
scissors
packaging tube
masking tape
pencil
paper
dressmaker's pin
silver-coloured adhesive tape

LEAFY HEART: Bend garden wire into a heart shape. Bend a loop at either end and hook the two together. Bind on twigs with florist's wire.

1 Cut a strip of foil approximately 15 x 5cm/6 x 2in. Wrap it round the packaging tube and secure with masking tape where the two ends meet. The foil will mould itself to the shape of the tube.

2 Draw and cut out a paper heart about 4cm/1½in high. Use a pin to pierce holes along the foil. Position the heart and pierce holes around it. Remove the foil and fold down the edges. Join the back with silver tape.

SIMPLY
NATURAL

———

Beautiful table settings are easy to create when you keep everything natural. Leaves and fibres, clays and woods that are happy together outdoors will be happy together indoors, too.

Here, the table is covered with hessian (burlap) – a robust version for the tablecloth, a finer, paler one to give the place mats greater definition. The fringed edges lend a soft finish, and the lines of beading add a decorative touch. Dried leaves pinned together with tiny lengths of wood make wonderful alternative place mats. Tassels of raffia make the most delicate of napkin rings, and earthenware vases and slipware crockery represent the earthy shades. Gold initials written on autumn leaves make innovative place names, while chocolate leaves add a delightful organic-inspired accompaniment for a fruit dessert such as lychees.

RIGHT: Let nature dictate the colour scheme using wood, natural undyed fibres and hand-made pottery.

LEAF PLACE MATS

These fine organic place mats are inspired by those used in the South Seas. The leaves are cleverly joined together by tiny "pins" of wood. To make the mats you will need strong, slightly flexible dried leaves which are available from dried flower specialists.

MATERIALS
dried leaves
small woody stems, cut into
1cm/½ in lengths

1 Work out a design by laying the leaves down on a flat surface, letting them overlap generously. You can make a circular mat by laying them in concentric circles or a rectangular mat by placing them in overlapping lines, any other shape you choose.

2 Fix the leaves together with the "pins", cut from dried stems. Use four wooden pins for each leaf. Adjust the leaves so they are flat.

CHOCOLATE LEAVES: Delicate leaves made from chocolate are pretty garnishes. Silk leaves provide the best moulds. Slowly melt the chocolate in a bowl set over a pan of boiling water. Draw each leaf lightly over the melted chocolate to coat one side and leave on a plate in the freezer. When the chocolate is set, carefully peel the leaf away. Keep the chocolate leaves in the freezer until you are ready to serve them.

RAFFIA TASSELS

Raffia, which is made from a variety of palm tree, is a wonderful organic material that ties well and withstands washing. It is easy to make raffia into napkin rings with tassels, which are perfect for this natural look. The long ends of the ties are plaited (braided) and used to tie around the napkins.

MATERIALS
raffia
scissors

1 Make a skein of raffia about half the thickness and double the length of the finished tassel. Tie a few strands of raffia tightly around the centre of the skein, leaving long ends for the plait (braid).

2 Fold the skein in half and tie a single piece of raffia near the top of the tassel. Trim the ends of the tassel. Divide the long ends at the top of the tassel into three, then plait them. Tie the plait around the napkin.

BEADY MATS: *Fray the edges of the place mats, then knot three wooden beads on to a length of string and stitch to each end.*

EASTER FESTIVITY

———

Let Easter take on an East European flavour. In that part of the world, the feast is traditionally celebrated with nature-inspired decorations and specially prepared foods. Here, violets set the colour scheme, combined with aqua, which happily mixes and matches in all its shades.

Spring branches hung with decorated eggs are a continental tradition, the branches bursting into leaf and blossom over the days of the celebration. Pussy willow branches are a charming alternative to blossom, creating a dramatic yet light and airy centrepiece. Violets are used in tiny posies as place ornaments and for decorating the traditional dome-shaped Easter cake and Russian cream cheese dessert, *pashka*. The pretty flowers are echoed in the tea cups and saucers. Painted eggs have been used as festive decorations throughout.

RIGHT: Violet and aqua make fresh alternatives to yellows as a spring colour scheme.

VIOLET POSIES

These delightful violet posies are easy to put together and make charming decorative party favours that guests will want to take home at the end of the festivities. The delicate flowers wilt once picked, so be sure to keep them in water (in tumblers, perhaps) until everyone is ready to leave.

MATERIALS
FOR EACH POSY:
3 long-stemmed leaves
15 violet blooms, tied with garden twine
23cm/9in turquoise ribbon
approximately 15cm/6in gauzy purple ribbon

1 Select long-stemmed leaves and place behind the violet flowers. Spiral-bind the bunch of flowers and leaves with the turquoise ribbon, as shown, and add a gauzy purple bow at the top, just under the violet blooms.

POTTED UP: Tiny mauve campanulas are displayed in a painted empty egg shell which has been rubbed over with a little iridescent pearl powder to catch the light. To finish, the egg shell stands in a simple china egg cup to make a delicate and whimsical display. Add a teaspoonful of water to the bottom of the egg shell for the flowers to drink.

EASTER EGG TREE

Any seasonal branches about to burst into bloom can be used for an Easter tree, hung with bought or home-decorated eggs.

MATERIALS
secateurs (pruners)
6 branches of pussy willow
vase
7 blown white eggs
white matt emulsion (latex) paint
and small artist's paintbrush
royal icing
piping (pastry) bag
assorted small cake decorations, such
as sugar flowers and mimosa balls
florist's medium-gauge wire
wire cutters
ribbon bows

AQUA EGGS: A basket of chocolate and decorated eggs makes a pretty display. Brush blown eggs with aqua paint mixed with iridescent pearl powder.

1 Cut the branches to length and place in a vase of water. Paint the eggs with white emulsion (latex) and allow to dry. Use royal icing to stick the cake decorations to the eggs.

2 Cut a wire 15cm/6in long and make a loop at one end. Thread through an egg and bend the loop flat against the bottom. Thread through a ribbon bow and make a hook for hanging.

THANKSGIVING

———

The wonderfully soft grey-greens and the mellow golds of winter squashes provide a subtle colour scheme for a Thanksgiving celebration. A pile of pumpkins forms a striking centrepiece, while small hollowed-out squashes become soup bowls. Dried oregano topiary trees offer fragrant focal points at either end of the table, and imitate the gently drying and falling leaves outside.

Real autumn leaves are cut to smaller leaf shapes and used as printing blocks to add decoration to a plain tablecloth. Runner (green) beans, symbolic of a fruitful harvest, are used as place decorations for the soup course, their soft green skins complementing the colours of the pumpkins and squashes. If the guests outnumber the available dining chairs, garden chairs can be "softened" or a disparate set of chairs can be co-ordinated by making button-on slips to fit over the backs.

RIGHT: Turn squashes into soup bowls and pumpkins into decorations to create an evocative autumn table.

SQUASH SOUP BOWLS

Squashes come in a wonderful array of shapes, sizes, and colours, ranging from pale green to rich autumnal red. Here, hollowed-out squashes make unusual seasonal soup bowls, and are especially appropriate for serving hot and delicious pumpkin soup. Add a pair of runner (green) beans beside each bowl for decoration.

MATERIALS
squashes
sharp kitchen knife
metal spoon

1 Cut the top third from each squash and a sliver from the bottom so that the soup bowl will stand flat. Using a metal spoon, carefully hollow out the seeds and enough of the flesh to create an attractive bowl shape to hold the soup.

PILE OF PUMPKINS: Pumpkins at varying stages of ripeness can be piled one on top of the other and sat on silver-grey reindeer moss for a pleasingly toned arrangement. For an evening party – especially at Hallowe'en – you could cut a "lid" from the top pumpkin, scoop out the seeds and flesh, and then cut decorative patterns in the skin, before placing night-lights (tea lights) inside.

LEAF-STENCILLED TABLECLOTH

This attractive idea is a witty way to hand-print a cloth with a seasonal motif. Use a real autumn leaf mounted on to a wood block or thick card (cardboard) as the printing block, in order to produce a veined effect.

MATERIALS
wooden leaf shape or thick card
(cardboard)
craft knife and cutting mat
clearly veined autumn leaf
all-purpose glue
cork
fabric paint
saucer
newspaper
tablecloth

2 Carefully cut out the leaf shape using a craft knife and cutting mat. Glue this real leaf to the wood block or the card template to use as a printing block.

3 Glue the cork to the other side to make a handle. Dip into a saucer of fabric paint and work off excess colour by stamping on to newspaper. Stamp on to the cloth at regular intervals.

1 Place the wooden leaf shape or card (cardboard) template on to a large autumn leaf. (For the template, draw a leaf shape on to the card and cut it out using a sharp craft knife and cutting mat.)

FRESH FLOWERS

The elegant lines of clean white orchid heads make for beautiful napkin ties – the perfect complement to pure white linen. Large green leaves set off the all-white design.

MATERIALS
FOR EACH NAPKIN:
25cm/10in narrow off-white ribbon
2 leaves
1 orchid head or other similar-size
white flower

BEAUTIFUL BOUQUET: This elegant bouquet of two types of white tulip was made especially for the table setting, but the bride's own bouquet could just as easily be put into a beautiful container after the ceremony, transforming it into an exquisite centrepiece.

1 Softly pleat the napkin to fit on the plate. If the napkin is too long make a large tuck in the centre, then pleat it into a fan.

2 Loosely tie the ribbon around the middle of the napkin. Carefully tuck the leaves into the ribbon, followed by the flower.

HEARTS AND RIBBONS

Frosting glasses is quick and easy, but the technique is all too often restricted to the rims. On romantic occasions, take the idea a step further by frosting a heart shape on the side of each glass. The delicate frosting is remarkably resilient and will last well throughout the festivities.

MATERIALS
2 saucers
1 egg white, beaten
small artist's paintbrush
glasses
caster (superfine) sugar
short lengths of off-white ribbon

TULLE GIFT: A square of white (net) tulle and tissue paper is cut and filled with silver sweets (candy), and tied with a white satin ribbon.

1 Dip the paintbrush into the beaten egg white and paint the outline of a heart shape on to the glass. You will not see much at this stage, but fill in the heart shape with plenty of egg white.

2 Immediately sprinkle caster (superfine) sugar on to the heart and shake off the excess. Dip the rim of the glass into the egg white, then into the caster sugar. Shake off the excess sugar. Decorate with a ribbon bow

TRADITIONAL CHRISTMAS

———

For a truly traditional Christmas, hark back to an era before the invention of tinsel and baubles when natural, organic materials provided the decoration, the textures and the evocative scents. Draw inspiration from the Elizabethans, who created a festive ambience rich with the aroma of oranges and bay leaves, and of heady spices such as cinnamon and cloves.

These ingredients can be the starting point of an elegant colour scheme, substituting russets and oranges for the more usual reds. Supplement the rich mood by looking for exotic fruits, flowers and vegetables such as pomegranates, Chinese lanterns and arti-chokes, and highlight them with voluptuous bunches of black grapes. Use rusty metal vases and rich brass or amber glass plates, then add a hint of gold.

RIGHT: At Christmas, let nature do the decorating, adding colour with fruit and flowers, and scent with spices and beeswax candles.

BROCADE PARTY FAVOURS

A charming brocade bag tied up with silk cord is gift enough indeed; fill it with a small present for each guest and place it decoratively next to each setting.

MATERIALS
FOR EACH BAG:
brocade, 15 x 60cm/6 x 24in
scissors
needle
thread
small gift
20cm/8in silk cord
rosebud (optional)

1 Cut two identical pieces of brocade, each measuring 15 x 30cm/6 x 12in. Fold down a 5cm/2in hem at the top edge of each piece, tuck the raw edge underneath. Stitch along the length of the hem.

2 With right sides facing, stitch around three sides, leaving the top edges open. Turn to the right side, fill with a small gift and tie the cord around the bag. Decorate with a rosebud if desired.

GOLDEN TASSELS: Dress elegantly etched glasses with golden tassels tied to the stems with golden twine to give them an air of celebration.

ADVENT CANDLES

1 Soak the florist's foam block in water and set it on a plate. Carefully push the candles into the foam.

2 Cut the tree ivy stems to size and push them into the florist's foam. Gild some of the berries with picture framer's gilt wax.

Traditionally, the four Advent candles are burned for an hour on each Sunday leading up to Christmas. On the first Sunday, one candle is burned for an hour. On the second Sunday it is burned alongside the second candle, and so on. This lovely idea inspired this table centrepiece, which could just as well have all candles burning on one occasion.

MATERIALS
florist's foam block
plate
4 church or beeswax candles
bunch of tree ivy, with berries
secateurs or scissors
picture framer's gilt wax
fine wire
wire cutters
10 Chinese lantern flowers

3 Pass a wire through the base of each Chinese lantern flower and then twist the ends together. Push the wire ends into the florist's foam base at intervals to hold the Chinese lanterns in position.

SEASONAL GARLAND

Natural decorations are by far the most beautiful. This easily made garland can be placed on a mantelpiece or adapted for use as a beautiful staircase decoration.

MATERIALS
plastic garland cradle or chicken wire, the length of desired finished piece and 3 times the width
wire cutters (optional)
3 florist's foam blocks
large bunch of tree ivy, with berries
florist's medium-gauge stub wires
picture framer's gilt wax

FOR EVERY 15CM/6IN OF GARLAND:
1 dried artichoke
2 dried oranges
cinnamon sticks
gold cord
scissors

1 First make the base. If using a garland cradle, fill each section with florist's foam, then soak in water. Join the cradle sections together. If using chicken wire, roll it into a long sausage filled with florist's foam and cut to size. Soak in water, then form into a circle. Push tree ivy sprigs into the foam to make a full base.

2 Pass a florist's wire through the base of each artichoke and orange, then insert them along the garland. Gild the ivy berries, the oranges and the tips of the artichoke leaves, using picture framer's gilt wax.

3 Tie the cinnamon sticks into bunches of two or three with gold cord. Pass a wire through the cord and then use this to insert each cinnamon bundle into the garland at regular intervals.

FORMAL URN ARRANGEMENT

Urns always give flower arrangements a dignified look and encourage the professional results. Choose some material that drapes gracefully, and some that gives structure to the arrangement. Here, russet roses and striking orange calla lilies are set against a background of rich green tree ivy with gilded berries.

MATERIALS
florist's foam block
scissors
metal urn
large bunch of tree ivy, with berries
secateurs (pruners)
picture framer's gilt wax
5 calla lilies
5 russet roses

1 Soak the florist's foam block in water. Cut it to fit the urn and place inside. Trim the tree ivy to length and gild the berries using the picture framer's gilt wax. Use the ivy to make a full base arrangement.

2 Trim the calla lilies to length and place them in the arrangement. Repeat with the roses to complete, making sure they are at slightly different angles.

MODERN CHRISTMAS

———

A sharp, modern Christmas table teams orange with burnished gold. Set against a strong structure of large, almost geometrical, but elegant shapes, there is scope for adding some tasteful embellishments with plenty of seasonal sparkle. A generously sized tall glass vase piled high with kumquats makes an unusual centrepiece and is balanced by a shallow stemmed dish containing shimmering orange and golden baubles. But the real ingenuity comes into play with the detail: glasses laced with fine gold wire, then given a golden stripe punctuated by glittering miniature jewels, and plates decorated with more jewels and gold-painted leaves.

Brass underplates topped by glass plates, together with brass cutlery and gold lustre coffee cups, add to the festive gold theme.

RIGHT: Give expression to the Christmas spirit by adding decorative treats, such as gift-wrapped party favours and foil-wrapped sweets (candy), to the table.

DECORATED GLASSES

Christmas is the time for decoration and embellishment, so dress your wine glasses for dinner. Lace fine gold wire around them, then add jewel-punctuated golden stripes and strings of gold beads to create simple yet striking decorations for glassware. A stick-on jewel added to the golden rim of each glass completes this lavish yet elegantly under-stated look.

MATERIALS
fine beading wire
stemmed glasses
all-purpose glue
masking tape
card (card stock)
gold spray paint
craft knife and cutting mat
steel ruler
stick-on jewels (rhinestones)

1 "Lace" the fine beading wire around the stem and bowl of a glass. Tie the wire to hold it in place, and add a spot of glue.

2 Stick a length of masking tape, (long enough to go around the glass) on to a piece of card (card stock) and spray it gold. Cut the tape into thin strips. Peel off a strip of tape and attach to the rim of each glass and add a stick-on jewel (rhinestone).

GOLDEN PLACE CARDS

Touches of gold will turn ordinary small cards available from stationers into seasonal place cards, decorated with gold-painted leaves.

MATERIALS
small, round-cornered cards
ruler
craft knife and cutting mat
gold pen
stick-on jewels (rhinestones)
stems of foliage
gold paint
small artist's paintbrush
all-purpose glue

1 Score across the mid-way point of the card using the ruler and craft knife. Fold the card. Write the guest's name on the front in gold, and add a stick-on jewel (rhinestone).

2 Paint the leaves on the foliage with gold paint, and use to decorate the card. Glue in place.

ORANGE TWIRLS: The simplest decorations enhance the modern theme. Here, a textured manilla card springs to life with a twirl of orange paper ribbon, used in gift wrapping. To make the ribbon twirl, run the edge of a closed pair of scissors along a short length and release. Glue the ribbon spiral lightly to the card for a stylish season's greeting. Sprinkle orange twirls over the table to give little accents of colour and vitality.

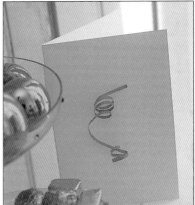

STARRY TABLECLOTH

A white voile overcloth can be given the Midas touch with the addition of simple six-pointed golden stars.

MATERIALS
circular object, about 7.5cm/3in
in diameter
card (card stock)
pencil
ruler
white voile to fit the table and hang
down the sides
gold paint
small artist's brush

FLOATING PETALS: Gerbera petals add co-ordinated decoration to a pretty glass finger bowl. You could use any type of petals, either keeping to one colour or using a range of shades for a really vibrant effect.

1 Place the circular object on the card (card stock) and draw around it. Draw three lines for the star to make six equal sections.

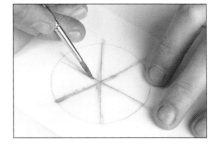

2 Place the card under the voile and carefully paint the star shape on the cloth, using gold paint. Repeat. Allow to dry.

GOLDEN GIFTS

Wrapping offers great scope for adding impact to co-ordinated table settings. These gold-painted white tissue parcels are a simple solution, and look highly effective in orange glass bowls.

MATERIALS
gifts
white tissue paper
gold paint
small artist's brush
gold organza ribbon
gold-painted leaves (as for Golden Place Cards)
fine gold ribbon

1 Wrap up each gift, then paint gold dots and strokes on the tissue paper parcel. Tie with organza ribbon, and decorate with gold leaves and fine gold ribbon.

GOLD ON GOLD: *This large pedestal bowl of Christmas tree baubles is reflected in a lower pedestal bowl of foil-wrapped sweets (candy) and a gold lustre coffee cup. Mix a few bronze or red baubles in with the pale gold to create colourful highlights. As Christmas Day extends into the evening, the firelight and artificial light will increase the sparkle.*

INDEX